I0411968

Prescription Drug Abuse

The Ultimate Cure Guide for How To Overcome A Prescription Drug Addiction

Table Of Contents

Introduction

First off, I really want to thank you for downloading this book. The pages in this book were developed through years of experiences that I have gone through, as well as what has proven to work for others that I have talked to and have researched. I also want to congratulate you for taking the time to understand your own prescription drug addiction and how you can overcome it.

I can guarantee that you will find this book useful if you make sure to implement what you learn in the following pages. The important thing is that you IMPLEMENT what you learn. A prescription drug addiction is not conquered overnight but the important thing to remember is that it is definitely possible for you to overcome it. What I am giving you is the information so that you can understand your own mind, how prescription drug addictions negatively affect those around you, as well as the steps you will need to make that journey.

Many people experience drug addictions and aren't really aware of the signs and symptoms that are going on. There is a difference between taking drugs that are prescribed to you and feeling the need to take a pill in order to function properly, even without the recommendation of your doctor.

As you go through these pages, you'll get a better understanding of what prescription drug addiction really is, the signs and symptoms of someone who has a prescription drug addiction and you will learn several ways that you can overcome it. We will dive into what is going on in your mind, how your body reacts to your triggers, how your environment can influence your well-being, as well as what work is required of you to get past the roadblocks you have.

I recommend that you take notes while you are reading this short book. This will ensure that you get the most out of the information in here. I want you to feel that you made a purchase that is worth your money and I want you to look over the notes of this book even after you've finished reading it. The notes will help you to pinpoint exactly what you need to implement and by writing things down, you will be able to recall specifics and how to handle certain situations when they arise.

Lastly, remember that everything in this book has been compiled through research, my own experiences, as well as the experiences of others, so feel free to question what you have read in this book. I encourage you to do your own research on the things that you want to look deeper into. The more you understand about your own mind and body, the better off you'll be. To overcome a prescription drug addiction in your life, it will take some work on your part but you can do it! So remember to read with confidence and an open mind!

Chapter 1:

What Is Prescription Drug Abuse?

When recommended by a doctor and taken as prescribed, prescription drugs can be beneficial in numerous ways. Prescription drug abuse is using a prescribed medication improperly and not using it based on the prescription of the physician. The intent behind the use of the prescription drug is to balance hormonal or chemical imbalances in the body that are causing issues for the person, either mentally or physically. Prescription drug abuse can be as simple as taking your friend's painkiller too often, to the injection of drugs with the use of a syringe or other methods.

This is an increasing problem among multiple generations. However, this is observed to be more common in young people and unfortunately, the combination of very loose guidelines for prescription drug companies, as well as the easy access for younger people through the expansion of technology, have made this such a trend.

There is a reason why there are prescribed dosages for certain drugs and why the prescription of the physician should be followed. Abuse of these types of drugs is not safe and can lead to dangerous long-term and short-term health problems. This may seem obvious to people on the outside looking in, however, we must remember that people who are addicted to prescription drugs are not usually in that clear of a headspace to be thinking so critically about their addictive behavior.

Some teens think that prescription drugs are generally safer to abuse because they are prescribed by doctors. This is a common misconception among teens and young adults. Taking prescription drugs for non-medical purposes can be just as dangerous as taking illegal drugs such as cocaine. Drug addiction is a process that can alter brain functions. Prolonged use of drugs can change the way the brain functions with long-term adverse effects.

There are a lot of pills that look the same. If you are not sure what it is or if it was prescribed to you by the doctor, then do not take it. You may have an adverse reaction to the drug, which can be fatal. Just because one drug works well for a person does not mean that it will be as effective for another. This is why doctors prescribe different drugs to different people, even if most of the symptoms may be the same. They must take allergies into account as well as other factors such as age, other health conditions, and strength of doses.

When Is There Prescription Drug Abuse?

Prescription drug abuse occurs when medication is taken in any of the following ways:

1. Consuming it without a prescription.

2. Consuming it in a way other than as prescribed.

3. Consuming it in order to get high or in combination with other drugs.

4. Consuming another person's prescription for pain relief.

Commonly Abused Prescription Drugs

The following drugs are often misused and taken for recreational use:

Depressants

These drugs work to slow down the functioning of the brain. Depressants include sedatives and tranquilizers - drugs that intend to calm and reduce anxiety.

Opioids and other derivatives of morphine

These are the usual painkillers that contain opium or substances similar to opium, that are used to relieve pain.

Stimulants

These drugs help to increase energy but, in doing so, can also increase heart rate and blood pressure.

Antidepressants

These are the drugs that are used on clinically depressed patients, but are also some of the most abused prescription drugs.

Why Do Some People Abuse Prescription Drugs?

Prescription drugs are often times easier to get as compared to street drugs because family members sometimes have prescription medications that can be easily accessed. Some people want to experiment with prescription drugs to help them lose weight, fit in, and have more fun.

Some people think that prescription drugs are less addicting and safer than street drugs. The truth of the matter is that these drugs are not safe to use if they are not intended for us. Those who try prescription drugs of family members and friends think that since these are prescribed, intake of such is not illegal. However, taking these drugs without any prescription and sharing them with others is not legal at all.

Chapter 2:

Signs, Symptoms And Effects

As mentioned earlier, taking prescription medication in a way other than what the physician has prescribed may be called prescription drug abuse. This can lead to addiction and may also result in various long-term and short-term adverse effects.

Depressants

These drugs are called "downers" and reduce the symptoms of mental illness. Some commonly used antidepressants are the following:

Xyprexa

Seroquel

Haldol

Xanax

Klonopin

Halcion

Librium

Short Term Effects:

Slowing down of brain functions, reduced concentration, lowered blood pressure, confusion, fatigue, slurring of speech, pupil dilation, lack of coordination, difficulty urinating, addiction, visual disturbances

Long Term Effects:

Depression, chronic fatigue, difficulty in breathing, sleep problems, anxiety or panic, rid for diabetes, weight gain, convulsion, hallucinations, delirium, high body temperature

Opioids and Morphine Derivatives

These drugs work to relieve pain and abuse can lead to dependence and symptoms of withdrawal. These are available in tablets, capsules and liquid forms. Some well-known brand names include:

Robitussin A-C

Roxanol

Demerol

Fiorional with Codeine

Percodan

Percocet

Tylox

Short Term Effects:

Nausea, coma, slowed breathing, drowsiness, constipation, unconsciousness

Long Term Effects:

Physical dependence, very addictive

Stimulants

Stimulants are also called "uppers" and can increase alertness and energy temporarily. Cocaine and amphetamines are the commonly used drugs in this category.

Short Term Effects:

Apathy, depression, exhaustion

Long Term Effects:

Addiction, feelings of hostility, paranoia, dangerously high body temperature, irregular heartbeat

Antidepressants

These drugs come in multicolored capsules and tablets. The following are the commonly abused antidepressants:

Prozac

Paxil

Celexa

Zoloft

Effexor

Remeron

Side Effects:

Irritability, suicidal thoughts, aggression, paranoia, hallucinations, insomnia, criminal behavior, tremors, nervousness and anxiety, irregular heartbeat, sweating, confusion, psychosis, inability to stay still

Other signs of prescription drug abuse may include the following:

Stealing prescriptions

Mood swings

Alteration in sleep patterns

Poor decision making

Unusually energetic and feeling high or sedated

Habitually losing prescriptions in order to get more

Getting multiple prescriptions from other physicians

When to see a doctor

If you think that you have a problem with prescription drug use, then it is important to see a doctor. If you feel embarrassed in seeing your physician, then there are other health care professionals who are willing to help you out. Addiction should be identified at the earliest possible stage, before it leads to more problems.

Remember, health care professionals are paid to answer your questions objectively so do not feel embarrassed to talk about your problem. They probably deal with people in a similar situation to yours on a daily basis.

Chapter 3:

Causes And Risk Factors

Both teenagers and young adults abuse prescription drugs for a variety of reasons. Some of the reasons are listed below:

Desire to avoid feeling painful situations

Wanting to get high

To relieve tension

To increase alertness and energy

To reduce appetite

Experimenting with the mental effects of the drug

Preventing withdrawal

Peer pressure and social acceptance or belongingness

Improving concentration and performance at school or work

Risk Factors:

Prescription drug users sometimes fear that they may become addicted to the drugs that they are taking for their medical condition, such as painkillers that are prescribed after a surgery. Patients who are taking addictive drugs as prescribed usually do not become addicted or abuse the drugs.

Risk factors for prescription drug abuse include the following:

Past or current addictions to alcohol or other substances

Teens or young adults in their early 20s

Those currently diagnosed with a psychiatric condition

Peer pressure that leads to drug use

Working in a health care environment where drugs are accessed easily

Improper knowledge about prescription drugs

Risk factors among adults

Prescription drug addiction among older adults is a growing risk because those who have various problems are taking in multiple drugs at the same time. This can lead to misuse and addiction because the pain in joints and muscles get more intense as we age.

Also, due to the unfortunate loneliness and isolation that some older adults face, the feelings that overdosing on drugs can bring may feel superior than living lonely and in pain.

Chapter 4:

How to Prepare for Your Appointment

A health care professional or your primary physician can help you overcome prescription drug abuse. But if you are addicted to prescription drugs, then the doctor may refer you to a specialist in drug addiction or a facility that helps people cope from drug withdrawal.

When you are preparing for an appointment, here are some things that you should:

1) Prepare a list of all the drugs that you are taking. Include the dosage and the frequency of the drug intake. If you are taking in over-the-counter drugs, then include them as well. Herbs and other supplements must also be included.

2) Write down any symptoms that you may be experiencing. This should be a comprehensive list and try to be as accurate as possible with your description of the symptoms.

3) If you have experienced a life changing event such as death or some other major stressors, then include them as well.

4) Write down the questions that you want to ask your doctor or health care professional.

If you are not yet able to think of questions to ask, these might help:

How long does the treatment last?

How long will it take before the treatment works?

What are my options for treatment?

What will happen to my other health issues when I undergo treatment?

Are there informative materials that I can read?

Are there websites that I can visit to help me during my treatment?

Your doctor may ask some questions and will also perform a physical exam.

Questions to expect are usually about the following:

Length of the problem

What could have brought about the addiction

Severity of symptoms

Any history of drug abuse, personally or within the family

Chapter 5:

Diagnosis and Treatment

Diagnosis

Signs and symptoms can provide clues to the doctors. Diagnosis can also be based on the history and the answers to the questions upon interview.

Blood tests and urine analysis can detect the presence of various types of substances. These can also be an indication in tracking the improvement of the patient undergoing treatment, over the long-term.

Treatment Options

Treatment options are given out on a case-to-case basis and may vary from one person to another. However, counseling or psychotherapy plays a major part in the treatment plan.

Counseling

Regardless of whether it is individual counseling or group counseling, counseling can have a profound effect in determining the factors that have contributed to the abuse of the prescription drug(s). During counseling, you will also learn how to fight the urge and avoid future drug abuse and relapse.

Counseling will teach you certain strategies in developing healthy relationships with others and determining positive ways of becoming involved in activities that are productive in the replacement of drugs.

Detoxification

Drug dependence and usage will determine if there is a need to detoxify. Detoxification can be a part of the whole treatment plan. Since withdrawal can be hazardous, the treatment plan has to be done under the supervision of a doctor.

Opioid Withdrawal

Symptoms of withdrawal may be comforted with strict and regulated doses of buprenorphine or methadone. Clonidine may be used to manage the symptoms of withdrawal as well.

Anxiolytic Withdrawal

Sedatives and anxiolytics use for an extended period of time may require weeks or months to wane off. The withdrawal symptoms may last for an even longer period, so the body will have to adjust to lower dosages at first, before finally going without medication.

This will take some time to get used to, so there are medications that are needed to stabilize the mood. Again, this is to be done under the strict observance of a doctor.

Withdrawal from Stimulants

Since there are no accepted medications yet to treat withdrawal from stimulants, treatment involves slowly reducing the medication so that withdrawal symptoms are eased.

While going to a medical professional is BY FAR the most important step in your recovery process, here are some steps you can take in your own personal life to help you to overcome a prescription drug addiction. Combined with professional help, using these guidelines will give you the best chance to overcome this addiction!

Avoid stressful situations with family and friends

This first one may seem obvious but it is one of the hardest for people to do. We spend most of our time around family and friends, and for many people this is the stimulus they need to avoid. Just because someone is your family or friend, it doesn't mean they are beneficial to your health.

You need to evaluate your friends and ask yourself, "Is this friendship helping me become a better person?" If the answer is no, this person may be causing stress in your life and you may just be used to dealing with it.

Even family can sometimes be unhealthy for you. Remember that if you are in a family situation that is not emotionally healthy, where you feel threatened or intimidated, this could very likely be the cause of your prescription drug abuse. Unfortunately, it is very common for teenagers to get involved with anti-depressants if they have a stressful relationship with one or both of their parents.

If you are unable to avoid the person you feel stressed out around, make sure to tell that person that you are uncomfortable when they act a certain way. It would be best to show them the trauma it has caused you, but it is ok if you do not feel comfortable with that. However, make sure to at least tell them that you would prefer them not to act that way around you because it makes you feel uncomfortable. Remember, they may have no idea what you are going through so don't hold back your feelings because the only person you are hurting in the long run is yourself.

Switch activities when you feel a stressful stimulus

When you notice yourself becoming stressed out in a certain situation, maybe you have a test coming up at school or a deadline approaching at work, do your best to find a healthy stress outlet that will help you to prepare for that situation. Good examples that have worked for people are using a stress ball that you can squeeze or even chewing gum.

Meditation

Mediation has been proven to help people who struggle with depression, anxiety, and stress. Meditating for 20 minutes a day can make a world of difference for someone who feels the need to consume a drug. The reason is, when you meditate, you clear your mind completely and it allows you to look at everything around you in a much more objective view.

You won't get as emotionally caught up in all the little stresses in your life, which will help you to pinpoint what you are getting stressed or worried about in the first place.

Meditation has made a huge difference in my own life and I always feel much less stressed out on the days that I do meditate compared to when I don't. When my stress levels are lower, my risk of taking a drug drops as well.

Eat a Paleo style diet and foods that encourage endorphin production

A Paleo diet is basically a diet that our caveman ancestors would eat. It doesn't contain any processed foods, just meats, beans, veggies, fruits, and anything that naturally grows from the ground. This can be very helpful to a someone who feels dependent on brain-altering drugs in multiple different ways.

First off, when your diet is filled with processed sugars and corn syrup, your brain doesn't function properly and can go into a "haze". This haze can sometimes prevent you from taking action on the important things in life and force you to stay in your current situation, even if you have the desire to make a change for the better. It is important to have a clear mind when trying to overcome such an addicting habit like prescription drugs.

Eat foods that encourage endorphin production. Endorphins are the chemicals in your brain that make you feel happy. These are the same chemicals that are released when a person has an orgasm, completes an important task, or helps someone they love. Eating a diet rich in foods that encourage endorphin production can really help you to be in a better mood, which will help you when you feel vulnerable and want to give in. Eating these types of foods is especially important when you know you may be facing a situation where you could get stressed out.

Here is a list of four foods that encourage endorphin production: vanilla, ginseng, chocolate (small amounts) and peppers. Blueberries also help your brain to function at its best.

Exercise

One of the most effective ways to improve general well-being is through physical exercise. First off, it improves cognitive functions, which lessen the triggers for one to indulge in drugs. It improves one's appearance and attitude towards life, making you feel more positive. When one has exercised, he/she is also able to manage his/her emotions much better.

It only takes a few minutes a day to exercise but the effects are invaluable. It is also worth pointing out that a large percentage of people who are addicted to prescription drugs live a sedentary lifestyle so the effects of exercising for these people, in particular, can make a world of difference.

Exercise also manages stress, which you may have otherwise taken out on yourself later that day. It even revives hormone levels, which helps keep the body and mind healthy and keep off excess weight. If you get into the habit of working out, you can tell yourself whenever you feel like taking a drug, you are going to take all of your stress out later that day on the weights at

the gym or running in the park. This has worked
wonders for me and many others.

Get enough sleep to think clearly

This goes along with your diet - not sleeping enough can cause major problems in your thinking. The last thing you want during the day is to become so tired that you aren't able to mentally keep yourself from popping a pill, due to low will-power. It would be so frustrating to stop taking the prescription drugs for a few days and then start again because you didn't get enough sleep the night before.

Sleeping also gives the body an opportunity to repair itself. For people with hormone and chemical dependencies, getting enough sleep makes sure that things balance out. Try to get at least seven to eight hours of sleep a night. Sleep is the best answer to stress, anxieties and other negative emotions. With proper sleep, one is able to manage different emotions with focus and presence of mind. Don't underestimate this one and cheat yourself.

Keeping your family, friends, or support network in the loop

I mentioned earlier that you don't NEED to tell your family and friends if you are not comfortable. I don't recommend telling them if you are not comfortable, however, your goal should be to ultimately tell the people that care about you sooner rather than later. The reason this is so important is that it creates some type of accountability for you to overcome the problem, as well as a small support system, even if it is just one person that knows about it.

No matter what we are trying to accomplish in life, if we are accountable to somebody else, it will always help us to accomplish that goal quicker because we can't just back out whenever we want. It is important to understand that no matter how bad the situation is, you are better off telling the people close to you because they are not going to care how bad it is, they want you to be happy.

Allow your family and close friends to be part of the healing process. Since the family comprises a person's immediate environment, it is only wise to make them a part of the treatment process. People with this issue clam up because of the judgment they might receive from the people around them. Although these reactions are sometimes valid, they inevitably trigger relapse.

If you can, find a group in your city or town with other people who suffer from prescription drug abuse. This is a great way to make friends who are dealing with the same issues as you are. This is also a great way to find an accountability partner if you are uncomfortable telling your family members.

Chapter 6:

Coping with Prescription Drug Abuse

Conquering prescription drug abuse is a very challenging task. It can trigger a lot of stress in the person trying to overcome it, as well as create difficulties for his/her family. This ordeal will require much support from friends, family, and even groups. You can approach the following for support during your treatment of prescription drug abuse:

Trusted circle of family and friends

Groups similar to Alcoholics Anonymous that have programs that you can adapt or follow

Religious organizations or church groups that aim to assist and help those who are on their way to recovery

School guidance counselors

Support groups in your local community (try to avoid online forums if possible, as a lot of misinformation can be found online)

Company assistance programs for employees, such as counseling for those who have drug abuse problems

Do not be embarrassed to solicit help from your friends and family members. The main hindrance is the fear of being judged, or that family and friends may get angry at you. However, looking at the bigger picture, people who genuinely care for you will help you out and accept you for who you are. They will go the extra mile to help you overcome a prescription drug addiction and will believe in you even when you may struggle to believe in yourself.

Helping a family member or friend

It may not be easy to confront another person about prescription drug abuse, especially if he or she is a close family member or a good friend. You will commonly encounter denial or anger. These are expected reactions and it is also normal that you will be hesitant about damaging your relationship. But it is important to help the family member or friend who is abusing prescription drugs before things get out of hand.

You have to be patient and understanding towards the person. Make sure that you make your concern and care known to that person. Encourage honesty and be there to help, if needed. If the person trusts you enough and has the internal motivation, then he/she will most likely take action on their situation. However, if the case worsens, then it is best to approach an expert.

It is not easy to help family members or close friends dealing with prescription drug abuse. They will usually not be willing to seek medical help despite them needing it badly. They will not see, at least at first, that what they are doing is harmful to them and the people around them.

Focus on telling the person about the positives that they will experience from overcoming their problem. Point out the negative affects in their life, but stay away from harping on the issue to the point that they will become angry at your presence in their life.

Intervention

Intervention is a process that is carefully planned out. This involves family or friends, or both, as well as concerned people who care about the person that is going through prescription drug abuse.

To have an effective intervention, it is important to consult an intervention specialist, addiction specialist, and a mental health therapist. They will all work together to help the person understand about the dangers of prescription drug abuse and ask them to agree to undergo treatment.

Preventing Prescription Drug Abuse

When you are prescribed a drug, it does not mean that you are at a high risk of drug abuse or addiction. Drug abuse does not happen often among those who are using sedatives, stimulants, or painkillers for their medical condition. But if you are taking a medication that is commonly abused, then here are some helpful tips for you to lower your risk of drug abuse:

See to it that you are getting the correct medication for your condition. When you visit your physician or health care provider, it is important that you are diagnosed correctly and that your symptoms are understood. Let your doctor know about all the other prescriptions that you have and any other medication that you are taking, such as over-the-counter drugs, herbs, and other supplements. You can also ask your physician if there is an alternative drug that you can take that has a lesser potential for addiction.

Make sure that you follow the directions carefully. Only use the medication based on the way that it was prescribed to you. Do not stop taking the medication unless you are otherwise instructed. Never change the dosage on your own without consulting your physician. If you have a painkiller that does not seem to relieve your pain, then do not take in more than the required dosage. Ask your doctor what you can do about it and wait for his/her prescription.

Talk with your doctor every now and then to make sure that the medication you are taking is working and that you are using the correct dosage that was prescribed to you.

It is important that you know the effects of the medication that you are taking before you consume it. Ask the physician or pharmacist about any effects of the drug, so that you will be familiar with what to expect.

When ordering medications online, make sure to look for a reliable pharmacy. There are online pharmacies that are selling counterfeit drugs that can be dangerous to your health. Make sure that you only order from a legit online pharmacy.

Chapter 7:

Abuse Among Teenagers

Every day, there are a lot of teens who are using prescription drugs without any guidance from a doctor. Many of them are doing this for the first time and some are using drugs for non-medical purposes. According to a survey done by Monitoring the Future on 2012, prescription drugs and OTCs are the most regularly abused drugs by 12th graders. Next in line is marijuana, alcohol, and tobacco.

Most of the teens and young adults have access to prescription drugs through their friends and relatives. They get these drugs without the knowledge of others because the drugs are readily seen and available at home.

Prescription drug abuse among teens stems from their desire to get the feeling of soaring, to treat pain, and sometimes they believe that it will make them perform better in class. Boys are usually inclined to abuse drugs to get high. Girls usually do it to lose weight and remain alert.

Signs and Symptoms

If you are a parent, then it is important to know and be aware of the signs and symptoms of prescription drug abuse, so you can immediately take action if your child suffers from it. Some of the most common are as follows:

Irregular schedule

Changes in circles of friends

Lack of interest in appearance, sports, and social activities

Missing cash and valuables at home

Sudden changes in mood

Being secretive

Increase in snoring

What can you do as a parent?

As busy as parents can be, it is vital to take notice of your child's performance in school and other activities. Stay up-to-date and show your child that you care by asking how his or her day went. Doing this every day can help you notice if there are any changes in your child's behavior, especially if he or she is in the teenage years. Here are some helpful tips for parents:

Educate yourself and know the possible signs and symptoms of prescription drug abuse among teenagers.

Increase awareness of your child's behavior and activities.

Keep your medications in a safe place. Lock it if necessary.

Monitor your medication so that you will know if a pill or two is missing.

If you have any unused medication then make sure to properly dispose of them.

Get to know the friends of your teenager. Find time to bond with him or her and see what the conversations are about.

Monitor online activity.

Do you need to monitor the online activity of your child?

To monitor or not to monitor? This decision lies entirely on the parents. Today, the internet is very accessible to all ages as long as you have a computer and an internet connection. Kids sometimes get past parental controls as they sometimes prove to be more tech-savvy than their parents.

As a parent, you need to know that prescription medications can easily be obtained online from both legitimate and rogue online pharmacies. The majority of the online pharmacies are operating illegally and they do not have a pharmacist. There are also a lot of counterfeit drugs and if your child gets ahold of these, there is no prediction of what to expect.

Teen Prescription Drug Abuse Prevention

Young people are at a relatively high risk for prescription drug abuse as compared to adults. Here are steps that you can follow to prevent it from happening:

Make sure to stress the dangers of prescription drug abuse to your teenage child. Let him/her know that even though it is prescribed by a doctor, it does not mean that anyone can take it. This is very important especially if your child has other current prescription medications.

Have rules for prescription drugs. Let your child know that sharing the prescription medication is a big no-no. It is illegal. Emphasize the weight of taking the dose as instructed by the doctor. Let your child know that he or she cannot make changes to the prescription.

Dispose of the medications in your home properly. Do not flush the drugs in the toilet unless your pharmacist says so. The local trash service may have a provision that accepts unopened or unused medications. If you are going to throw unused medicines in your trash at home, then remove them from the container and mix them with coffee grounds, along with some other unwanted substances. As for the container, remove and destroy the label before throwing it out.

Conclusion

I worked hard on creating the best guide for "overcoming a prescription drug addiction" that I could. These are all the strategies and information that has worked for me, as well as others that I have talked to and researched. I guarantee if you stay consistent they will work for you as well. Be optimistic about your current situation and make small progress each day!

If you feel like you learned something from this book, please take the time to share your thoughts with me by sending me a message. I would really appreciate it! Feel free to leave a review on Amazon as well.

Thank you and good luck in your journey!